ROBERT. M. DRAKE

beautiful CHAOS

Forever.

Forever does not seem too far
away. Sometimes it is after
we have lost someone when
we learn to love. Where hope
and dreams greet and everything
is beautifully perfect the way
it was meant to be. So hear me,
soon enough we will meet again,
old friend.

Don't worry.

Do not worry, little heart. They are
only feelings. So care a little less,
the ride will be much more than what
it seems.

Keep looking.

Look deeper through the telescope
and do not be afraid when the stars
collide towards the darkness,
because sometimes the most beautiful
things begin in chaos.

All is lost here.

Oh sweet child, but we are
all lost here! So close those
eyes and follow where your
heart leads.

Just a little push.

All she needed was a little push, to feather into the arms of the one she loved.

Between the sea and the sky.

It is written between the sea and the sky, within the horizon rest, that word. The word neither science nor religion can make sense of. The word to end or start all wars, the word we use to express something greater than ourselves. The word we die for, we live for and ironically look for when it cannot be seen. It is written on pillows so we dream of it and written over the stars so we can wish for it. So when we look closer, just a little bit closer, we discover it has always been within us. Buried deep inside our biology, our existence, just look a little closer - for all that we are and all that we will ever be is love.

Devour.

Devour me with the rawness; shred me down to the end of me. Grab me, bite me, destroy me and never fade so sweetly into the dark. Swallow me with aggressive gulps, twist me, crush me, break me down and expose my darkness to the twinkles which remain beneath the black above us. And when it is all over I will still crave you for all that you are.

Fall in love.

I want us to fall in love like drops of rain.
Grow in love like we grow through life
and never look back, like we left nothing
behind. Just us forever, floating through the
blackness of the infinite.

Call my own.

Your sky is full of stars and my arms too
short to reach a piece to call my own.

Fall apart.

Things were falling apart. We just could not slow down. We were evolving into something greater, perhaps too much for our own good. And one thing always remained as I moved on. I saved a little bit of love just in case you would ever return home.

Let us go.

Come away with me. Let us go somewhere. You and me, just the two of us! Let us wander through darkness, forget our worries and do all the things today that will help carve a better tomorrow.

Explore.

Always explore the world with new eyes,
dream of places you have never imagined
and discover a love so perfect it was almost
not meant to be.

Every night.

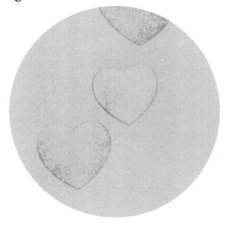

Every night I was going back to the strands of our memories and some nights, no every night, I would surrender to the fabric of you, because one night was not enough. I always found myself wanting more.

Not like you.

Dear God, I am not like you. I am weak, my bones brittle, my heart filled with darkness and at times my demons crawl out from the walls you helped me build. I am just an extension of your brilliance but what would it be like to be a wave in the ocean of you. I am lost in your shine and I drown in your touch. So maybe I have ignored you lately but this is me reminding you that I, too, suffer and I, too, seek the beauty in humanity. So hear me, you are not alone.

Rid me.

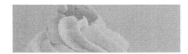

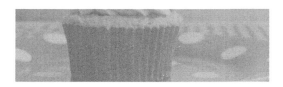

Rid me of all that has ever ruined me and
this darkness that consumes the life in me.
Rid me of brokenness and even wholeness.
Rid me of all the things that fill you empty.
Rid me in pieces, rid me to nothing but
leave just a bit for me to grow. Rid me to rid
me in you and not a second less, fill me with
all that makes you expand in such a small
space. So, that the best of me spills over you
and leaves not a trace to spoil.

Cycle.

I will be your spring if you will be my summer and I will be your fall if you will be my winter. We will cycle and cycle until forever breaks the seconds and the seconds define us for every moment we spend.

Too human.

Maybe we are too human and disaster trails behind us. I never understood us, for how can something so beautiful cause so much pain after all?

Words.

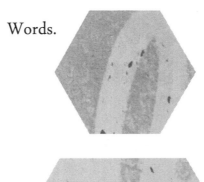

She said I had a way with words and I said she had a way with laughter. It spoke to me the way imagination speaks to a child, inspiring.

Make you beautiful.

Sometimes you have to shatter the mirror in you, to see all the pieces that make you beautiful.

Broke.

I broke myself beautiful when I left you; it was me saving me from myself.

Funny way.

Conquer the demons in you before letting
the demons in others conquer you.

The world.

Be authentic to yourself, but if you must cheat, cheat yourself out of the lies the world created.

Drizzle.

I am slowly falling apart, scorching away.
My ashes drizzle and I have destroyed myself
to wind over your shore, to remind you that
someone out there still burns for you.

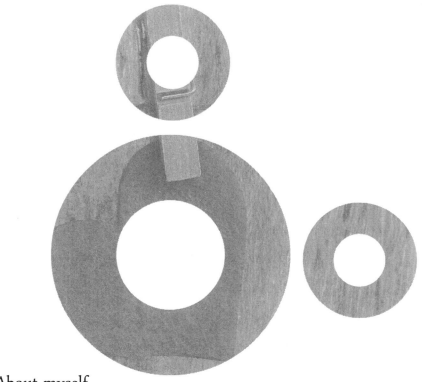

About myself.

And loving you was a pattern of
self-discovery because some way, somehow I
always ended up learning something new
about myself.

A million pieces.

I would break into a million pieces, if only it meant a million pieces of me to call your own.

Being burned.

I was married to the idea of loving her.
She sold it too well. The words
"I love you" felt like being burned alive
and it hurt but I swallowed the pain over
and over to slumber in the field of her,
without wake. Just dreaming, dreaming
of how my world would be without her,
too incomplete.

 charge in me.

 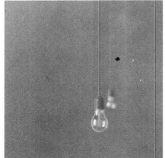

There is a charge in me that burns for you. I crave to recover all of you, all the pieces and peel away all that sours you. So do not be afraid when I give you all my years, my hours and my seconds because every moment finding you will be every moment finding myself as well.

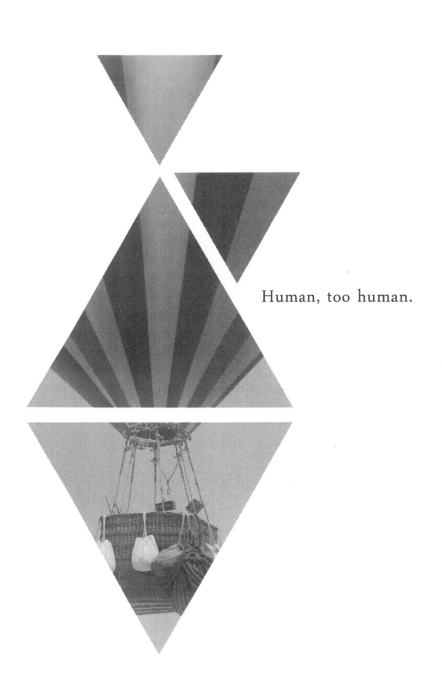

Human, too human.

She went on and became human, too
human. She alone accepted all of her
faults and in the end she was good,
enough to keep her smile on
permanently.

Violently missing you.

I am violently missing you and it kills me
that you linger so close. I will never be at
ease while watching the sunset, knowing our
stories will never end with the same words.
All sunsets have their own story, it is just
that ours will always fall incomplete.

Madness.

A touch of madness will always be stored in the crater of love.

Magic Moments.

And every magic moment brought
her closer to her dreams.

Burn away.

Burn away and burn every burning sorrow
that burns you like a burning star and
awaken all that you would burn for to burn
away every burning scar.

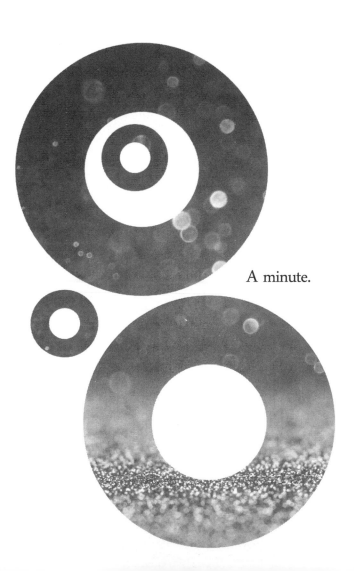

A minute.

All she needed was a minute to fall in love with the stars and after that night everything changed.

Sometimes.

Sometimes I feel like I do not know myself like I'm lost inside myself. And I cannot even live within myself and I cannot trust myself when I'm by myself. Too many broken pieces scattered of myself, too empty and maybe I'm not myself. I think I need you to save me from myself because without you I'm just not myself.

Danger.

Danger will always chase her and she will always greet it with a smile.

Please understand.

Please understand that without you I cannot finish the day. I cannot rest buried only in light. I too, need darkness to close my eyes and dream. I, too, need to feel the coldness of the night and I, too, need the stars to lamp over my sleepy eyes. I cannot find the words to describe why I need you. I need you like the day needs the night. That alone is enough to define everything of everything that I have kept buried beneath for so long.

Always.

You will always be beautiful, before and after today and when our days have seen age, all that once was will always remain.

Imagine.

Imagine what we would accomplish together
if we left our egos at the door.

We both saw ourselves.

She said she loved the ocean and I said I loved the stars and for the first time we agreed on something. We both saw ourselves loving the things we dreamed of, and ignored everything that made us beautiful.

Behind.

So laugh a little more, care a little more
and love a little more for all we will ever
be is what we become, and in the end we
become what we leave behind.

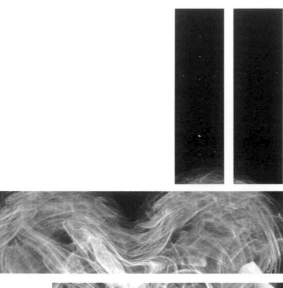

Fools rush in.

Let us go to a place where no one knows
us and find our smiles. Let us go to a place
where we can wander and find our laughter.
Let us go to a place where we can find
ourselves and find innocence. Let us go to
a place where we can fall and find a love
to catch us and take us to a place where
only fools rush in.

Footprints.

Maybe all the broken dreams and empty promises the world offered are just reflections of what is within us. Maybe one day we will learn to accept ourselves for all the faults sleeping beneath the footprints we leave behind.

Myself without you.

I know it is late but come away with me.
Let us run away in the dark and I promise
you, I will never see myself without you
again.

Belong.

We all could be great and leave our dreams on the shore. Drift away and still believe the best is yet to come. And even after everything, even after the tide brings us back to where we end, I would still feel empty knowing we drifted apart and you are only an ocean away from being where you belong.

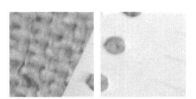

Felt lost.

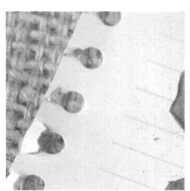

She always felt lost and it was beautiful not knowing how she would find herself. For everything she knew was a speck of something greater and it was just a matter of time until all of her made sense.

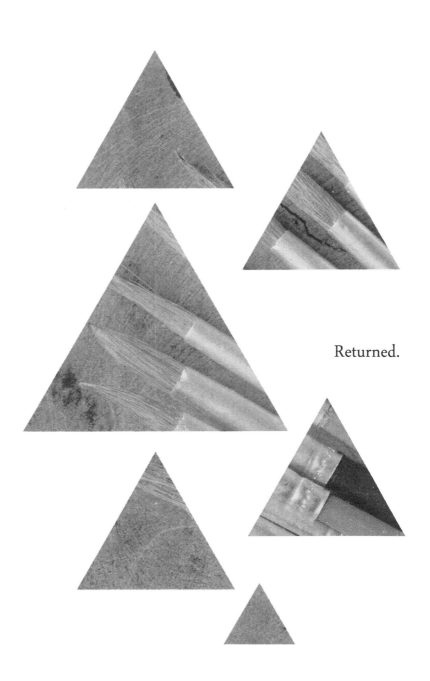

Returned.

He returned to her and his lips awakened every atom in her body. His love exhausted her stars, she could not help it! She stumbled and lost her balance, wrapped herself in his moonlight and forever she seasoned his love.

The wind.

Maybe her story does not have an ending.
Maybe God will remember her and wheel her
through the air, so we can all breathe her in
and exhale her brilliance through the wind.

Wild things.

We are beautiful things, wild things,
searching for the brilliance within us.

Feels like the sunset.

Cause missing you feels like the sunset and not a night goes by where I walk towards the shore, wishing you would shipwreck and just stay home.

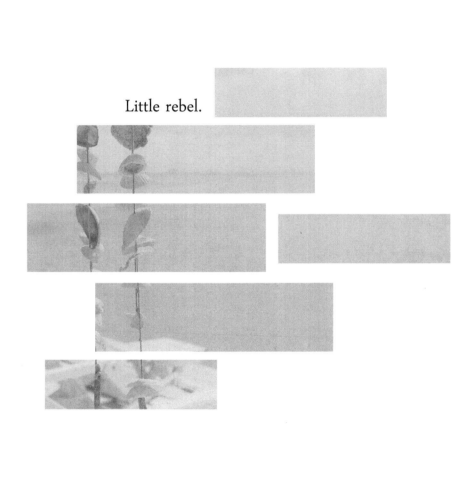

Little rebel.

She had a little rebel in her, a little chaos and
a little gentleness. She did not say much and
sometimes she would doze off. She would
drift away, dream with the stars and that was
ok. She had a little fight in her and every
time she built enough courage her voice would
echo through the sky. She was not complete
but she had enough. There was a science to
her genius, her madness, her beauty and there
was nothing she could not accomplish. She was
unstoppable and everything she ever wanted
she took, with nothing on but a smile.

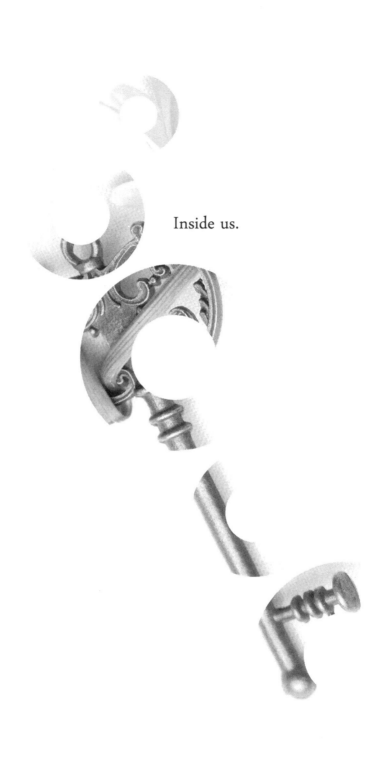

Inside us.

There was too much inside us. Maybe it was love or maybe it was something else. We had a light, a brilliance we tried so hard to ignore and all our faults had little significance to the story we were not willing to let go.

Dear you.

Dear God,

Every gust of wind carries your
voice. Every sunrise radiates the warmth
derailing from your smile. Every ocean
reflects the shades seasoning from your eyes
and during the night I can see everything
you have ever wanted me to see. Every star
exhales your favorite stories, wrapped in a
fabric of dreams. Every mountain, summit
top and meadow reminds me of your
scripting skin. And I know you, too, are
broken and every living thing that breathes
your voice, feels your smile, vessels in your
eyes, runs through your skin and looks up at
the sky to understand your story, has a little
piece of you inside them to call their own.

One day.

One day someone will inspire you and a love will chalk over your walls and the sun will love you and follow you. You will walk in sunshine. And you, too, will inspire and continue to be inspired and you will never destroy these moments where you and the light meet. You will never end.

Become it.

The more she went on to forget love, the
closer she went on to become it.

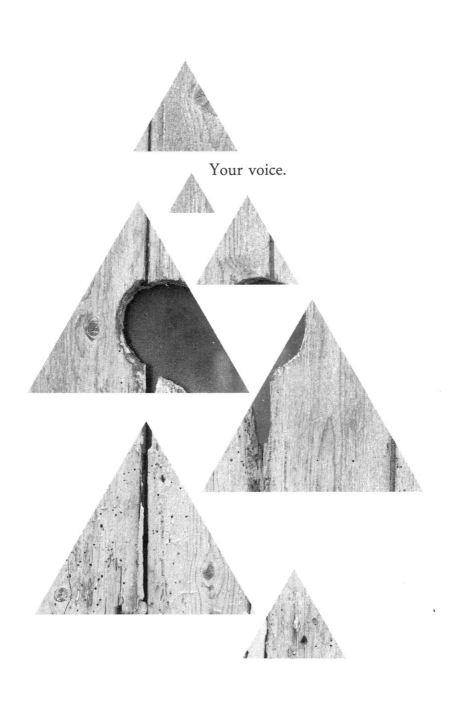

Your voice.

In your voice, I can hear a hundred years of music. A thousand years of the stars colliding, and a million years of everything beyond, pulsating through the vibrations of your soul. I have been listening, listening to all of you come together and now I understand why we are vessels submerged in greatness, because I have always drowned in you and forever I will run in the only place where I know I can breathe.

Learn.

We all can learn how to breathe submerged; we just have to find that one person worth drowning for.

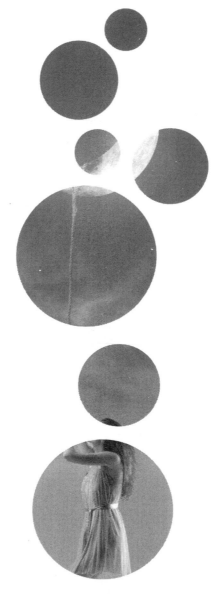

Awaken.

Stop looking for something when something has already found you. You have been living with your eyes closed. Awaken, it's there. Take it, it's yours.

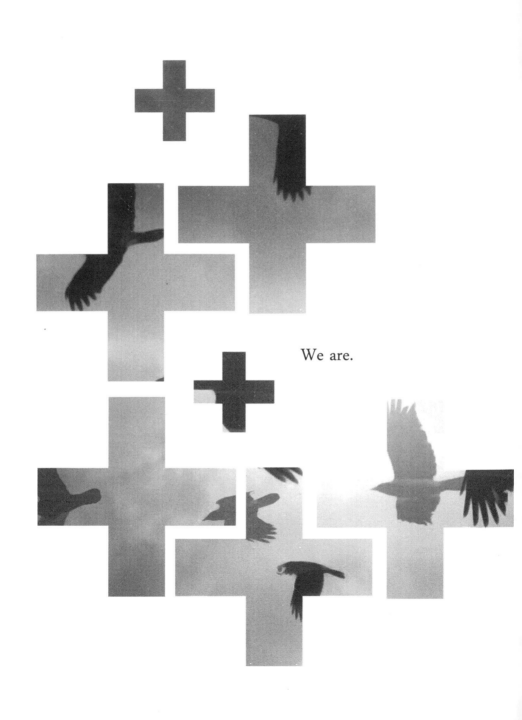

We are.

We are 93 million miles from the sun.
238 thousand miles from the moon.
A moment from finding magic and
one kiss away from reaching our
dreams.

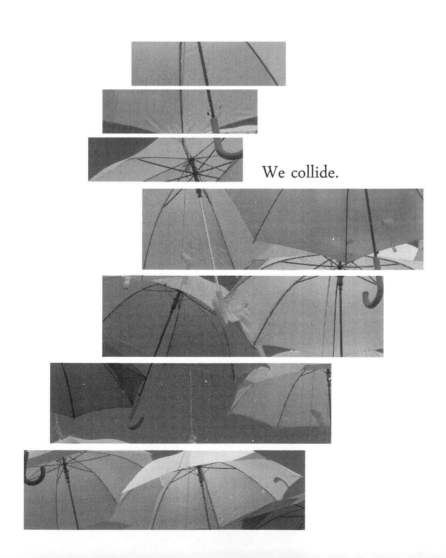

We collide.

You will be the clouds and I will be the sky.
You will be the ocean and I will be the shore.
You will be the trees and I will be the wind.
You will be the stars and I will be the moon.
You will be the sunset and I will be the horizon.
Whatever we are,
you and I will always, always collide.

Little heart.

O little heart, keep your smile youthful and never let go of love when the wind calls your name.

Beautiful things.

Let your love flow where the beautiful things
are and something beautiful will always come
your way.

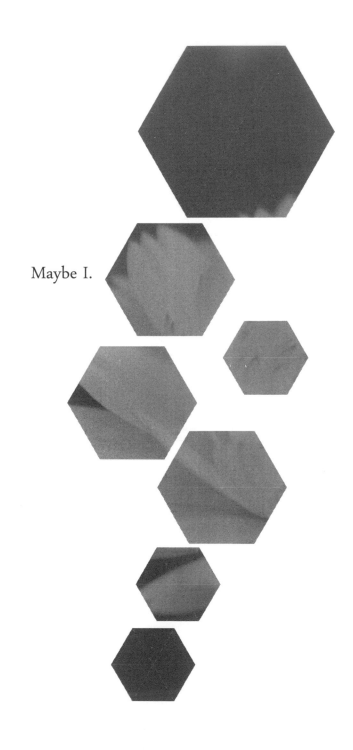

Maybe I.

Maybe I love too much and
maybe I show it too little.

Dreaming on the moon.

We are like astronauts, dreaming on the moon, telescoping the stars, exploring the skies and searching for the moments that take our breath away.

You will meet.

Somewhere someone is thinking of you.
Wishing one day somewhere somehow you
will meet.

Too many little.

She destroyed herself, too many little thoughts.
She fell apart, too many little pieces.
She wrote herself, too many little words.
She lost herself, too many little places.
She fell in love, too many little feelings.
She discovered herself, too many little stars.
She believed, too many little moments.
And in the end, she was home, too many
little things that reminded her of him.

Think you are.

You are only as free as you think you are
and freedom will always be as real as you
believe it to be.

We began to believe.

I taught her how to dream and she taught
me how to love and we saved each other
the moment we began to believe.

The stars.

Do not promise her the stars if you cannot see them yourself and never tell her you love her if love does not mean the world to you.

Welcome you home.

One day you will make peace with your demons and the chaos in your heart will settle flat. And maybe for the first time in your life, life will smile right back at you and welcome you home.

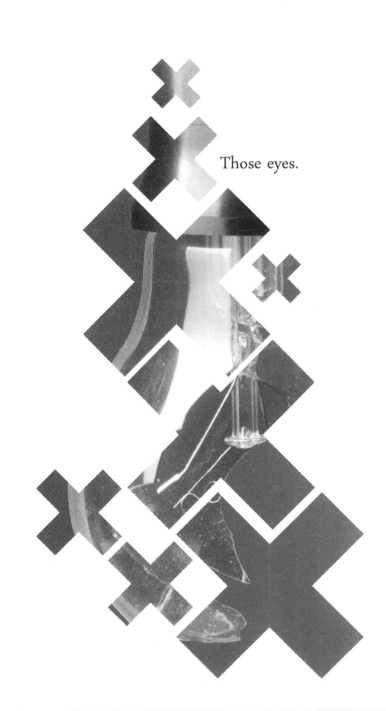

Those eyes.

Those eyes have seen so many places and that heart has felt so many things and yet you still smile at the darkest feelings and find expression in everything that is colored beautiful.

Beyond the ordinary.

We cannot deny the brilliance rooted deeply
within us and these moments that break
us and introduce us to something beyond the
ordinary.

She was.

She was a lot like the ocean, a lot like the wind and a lot like the stars. She taught me how to drown and feel things above the sky.

If loving you.

If loving you kills me tonight, then I was
ready for death the moment you said hello.

Sometimes I do not.

Sometimes I do not feel and sometimes I think too differently. I do not belong because I cannot find myself and I am sorry my heart is not big enough for you to call it home, when I cannot even say that for myself.

If we.

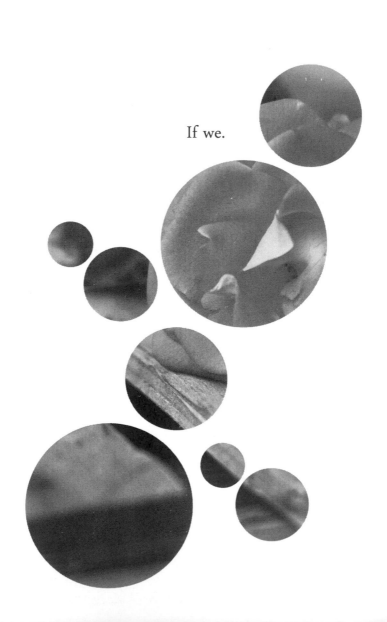

If we move too fast, we will break things.
If we move too slow, we will miss things.
And if we do not move at all, we will not
see things for how beautiful they truly are.

Maybe tomorrow.

Maybe tomorrow that goodbye will lead to a new hello, and maybe this time you will fuel the fire in her heart and make her stay.

We are magic.

We are magic.
We are moments.
We are dreams
and we are memories.
We are everything.
And in the depths
we swim deeper to discover
that we are not born whole
so we cannot be broken.
We are born in twos,
and we are searching,
searching for the other piece,
that other person
to guide us home.

Smile.

But there is so much to smile about, so why waste your time wiping down those tears.

Too much.

There is too much noise in me and too often I feel interrupted. I need order, I need love, I need all of you to calm the waves. All of you to set me free and all of you for all of me.

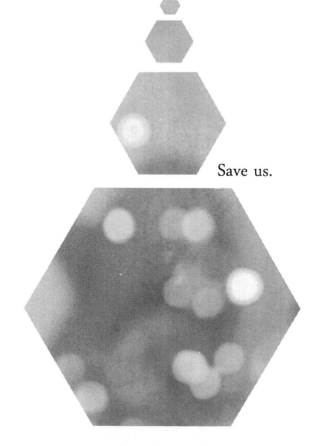

Save us.

To save us from them, we must separate ourselves. And to be different, we must question everything that makes us who we are.

Too much.

There is too much fuel in her. The world ignites her fire and she works both ways. When she loves, she loves too much and when she hates, she hates too much. And in between there is so much wage, so much that she loses herself in these moments. And the closer she was, the further apart she wanted to be. She just could not get it together, until she met him.

Hate is heavy.

I need you to understand that hate is heavy
so put it down. No, burn it down, burn it
all down and leave regret beneath its ashes.
So when the fire in your heart sparks,
everything you will do will burn bright and
hot. The world will never cease to ignore
the stars in you.

Brokenness.

Bind my brokenness; there is too much separation in me. Leave my scars but iron out the pain. Kill my darling memories, kill them all. So by morning I can dock a new sun and shine with only you.

Leave your heart little.

She left her heart little. She left her heart childish. And for her, every little moment felt like butterflies. She did not want to believe there was an end to love. So she drowned in the seconds beneath the moment where magic and stillness collide. And every time she looked into his eyes, she was reminded of how it felt to be alive.

This book is dedicated to Charise. May her flame live on within my heart and continue to inspire me every waking hour.

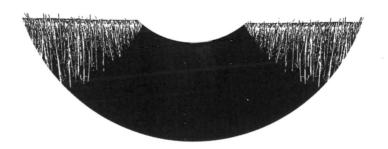

with open eyes, i see the world.
with an open heart i see the souls.
and with an open mind i see it all differently.

Thank you for your time.

Robert. M. Drake.

GRAVITY

A Novel by Robert M. Drake

Coming Soon...

ALSO AVALIABLE

ROBERT M. DRAKE
SPACESHIP

ALSO AVALIABLE

ROBERT M. DRAKE
SCIENCE

ROBERT. M. DRAKE

beautiful
CHAOS